Lenin as Election Campaign Manager

In recent years much criticism has been leveled against the participation of revolutionary socialists in capitalist elections. Almost all ultraleft organizations and many ultraleft individuals, including sincere but inexperienced radicals, denounce such activity. For example, in an editorial written just before the November 1968 elections, the *Guardian* (which often adapts to ultraleftism) stated, "we find it impossible to support anyone for any elected office within the government of International Murder, Incorporated." In order to reinforce this point, the editorial calls on Lenin for support. Agreeing with Lenin that there are times when running in elections might be useful, the editorial adds, "We also agree with Lenin that it's sometimes useful,

This pamphlet is based on a talk given to a Socialist Activists and Educational Conference held in Oberlin, Ohio, August 9–16, 1970. Doug Jenness, a longtime leader of the Socialist Workers Party, was its assistant national campaign director in 1968 and national campaign director in 1976 and 1988. He is editor of *An Action Program to Confront the Coming Economic Crisis* and author of *Farmers Face the Crisis of the 1990s,* both published by Pathfinder.

and even essential, to reject parliamentary reform. This is one of those times." This attempt to strengthen a weak case by distorted and disjointed references to the writings of a great revolutionary like Lenin is a common practice among these ultra-lefts.

In order to understand the revolutionary socialist approach to capitalist elections, we must untangle a web of misunderstanding and falsification of the history of the Marxist view, particularly Lenin's view, of electoral strategy. Is it true, as the *Guardian* indicates, that there were times when Lenin thought it useful to run in elections, while at other times he favored boycotting the elections? Did he place greater emphasis on boycotts or on participation in the electoral arena? Under what circumstances did he advocate these various tactics?

Before discussing Lenin's viewpoint and the experience of the Bolshevik Party, it would be useful to review Marx and Engels's thinking on socialist electoral activity.

Marx and Engels were ardent champions of universal suffrage and strongly supported all struggles to extend the right to vote in capitalist elections, particularly to the working class. They had no illusions, however, that the extension of suffrage would be the means by which the working class would win political power.

According to Engels, "the possessing class rules directly through the medium of universal suffrage. As long as the oppressed class, in our case, therefore, the proletariat, is not yet ripe to emancipate itself, it will in its majority regard the existing order of society as the only one possible and, politically, will form the tail of the capitalist class, its extreme left wing."[1]

But if universal suffrage is employed as a means of deception by the capitalist rulers, what possible use can it have for the revolutionary workers movement? Engels answers this ques-

---

1. Frederick Engels, *The Origin of the Family, Private Property, and the State* (New York: Pathfinder, 1972), p. 218.

tion, writing in 1895 about the situation in Germany at that time:

> The franchise has been . . . transformed by them [the workers] from a means of deception, which it was before, into an instrument of emancipation. And if universal suffrage had offered no other advantage than that it allowed us to count our numbers every three years; that by the regularly established, unexpectedly rapid rise in our vote it increased in equal measure the workers' certainty of victory and the dismay of their opponents, and so became our best means of propaganda; that it accurately informed us concerning our own strength and that of all opposing parties, and thereby provided us with a measure of proportion second to none for our actions, safeguarding us from untimely timidity as much as from untimely foolhardiness—if this had been the only advantage we gained from the suffrage, it would still have been much more than enough.

> But it did more than this by far. In election propaganda it provided us with a means, second to none, of getting in touch with the masses of the people where they still stand aloof from us; of forcing all parties to defend their views and actions against our attacks before all the people; and, further, it provided our representatives in the Reichstag with a platform from which they could speak to their opponents in parliament, and to the masses outside, with quite different authority and freedom than in the press or at meetings. . . .

> "It was found that the state institutions, in which the rule of the bourgeoisie is organized, offer the working class still further levers to fight these very state institutions. The workers took part in elections to particular diets, to municipal councils and to trade courts; they contested with the bourgeoisie every post in the occupation of which a sufficient part of the proletariat had a say. And so it happened that the bourgeoisie and the government came to be much more afraid of

the legal than of the illegal action of the workers' party, of the results of elections than of those of rebellion.[2]

Engels goes on to say that in the last decades of the nineteenth century in Germany, electoral propaganda was a more effective means of struggle than "revolutionary" adventures "carried through by small conscious minorities at the head of masses lacking consciousness"—referring to various ultraleft attempts by small groups to seize power through street fighting.[3]

In the same article he explains that through its electoral strategy, the Social Democratic Party of Germany grew rapidly despite the imposition of the Anti-Socialist Law by the Bismarck government. (From 1878 to 1890 the party had to function without a newspaper, without a legal organization, and without the right of combination and assembly.)

What are the key lessons from Engels's observations of socialist election policy in Germany? He viewed the participation of socialists in elections as "one of the sharpest weapons" to fight the state institutions and to expose the other parties before the masses; as an effective method of reaching the masses of people with the ideas of the party; as a useful platform to express the ideas of the party and attack its opponents if the party succeeded in winning seats; as a gauge of the strength and support of the party among the masses; and as a means of legitimizing the party before the masses and putting it in a position where attempts to outlaw the party could be fought more easily. This was particularly important in Germany in light of the Anti-Socialist Law. The party's legal activities—its election campaigns—were powerful weapons enabling it to fight for the right of the party to exist.

Because of the relatively peaceful development of German

2. Engels, "Introduction to Karl Marx's 'The Class Struggles in France: 1848-1850,'" *Collected Works* (hereafter *CW*) New York: International Publishers, 1975–), vol. 27, p. 516.
3. Engels, *CW*, vol. 27, p. 520.

capitalism and the mighty advance of its productive forces in the absence of any major revolutionary situations, large sections of the German Social Democratic Party gradually adapted to capitalism and became reformist. As a consequence, the parliamentary activity of the German Social Democratic Party took on an entirely different form from that outlined by Engels. Socialists in the Reichstag began to view parliamentary activity not as a valuable method of agitation and propaganda, but as a means of winning legislative reforms and advancing their own parliamentary careers. A similar phenomenon was also occurring in France and other European countries. Parliamentary tactics were no longer seen as part of the mass struggle against capitalism. Election campaigns were viewed as a means of reforming capitalism.

In the United States before the First World War, one wing of the Socialist Party under the leadership of Eugene V. Debs made excellent propaganda use of capitalist elections—a magnificent example from which we can learn a great deal. But there was also a very large reformist section of the party that sought seats and careers in the capitalist government, primarily municipal governments, in order to carry out a few minimal reforms—such as fixing up a sewer system. "Sewer Socialists" is what they were aptly called by the revolutionists of that time.

As this parliamentary careerism deepened and became stronger in Western Europe and the United States, Lenin, basing himself on the revolutionary traditions of Marx and Engels, was creatively enriching the revolutionary socialist approach to electoral strategy. The first experience of the Bolshevik Party with elections was in 1905 when the tsarist regime attempted to call elections for the Duma—the Russian name for parliament. (It wasn't a parliament like those of Western Europe because Russia was not a bourgeois republic. Russia was ruled by a tsarist monarchy which was making a concession to the revolutionary upsurge by having a form of parliament, with the aim, however, of maintaining the monarchy.)

The Bolsheviks utilized the tactic of boycotting the elections to the Duma, and the Duma was swept away by a general strike in October 1905. The tactic was obviously successful, and Lenin later so analyzed it. The boycott was consistent with the objective conditions and the revolutionary possibilities in the country at the time, which made it wrong to rely on the parliamentary tactics of a more stable period.

In 1906, when elections were called again, the Bolsheviks again boycotted the election. Later, Lenin admitted that this boycott had been an error. The Bolsheviks had failed to recognize the ebbing of the revolutionary upsurge as soon as they should have, and to make the necessary tactical adjustments. It was a minor tactical error, Lenin wrote, but an error nonetheless. The Bolshevik boycott did not succeed in sweeping aside these elections and the Duma was established. In a few months the tsarist government felt it was necessary to disband this Duma and set up a new one that would be more loyal. The government called for new elections in early 1907. This time the Bolsheviks and the Mensheviks joined with other radical parties in running candidates in the election. A number of Bolsheviks were elected to office as deputies in the second Duma.

In June 1907 the second Duma was dissolved, smashed by a coup d'état, and the Social Democratic deputies were arrested and imprisoned. New elections were called for November 1907. At this time a strong ultraleft faction within the Russian Social Democratic Labor Party (to which both the Bolsheviks and the Mensheviks belonged), embracing the majority of the leadership of the Bolshevik organization, took the position that these elections should be boycotted. On the basis of the experience of the second Duma, which had been smashed, and the successful boycott in 1905, they said that the party should not participate in these elections.

Lenin was the only central leader of the Bolsheviks who favored participation in these elections. The ultraleft Bolsheviks were defeated, and the party ran candidates, with the Bolsheviks having a few deputies elected to the third Duma.

The third Duma lasted until 1912, when elections were called again, for a fourth Duma—the last Duma before the February 1917 revolution.

Because there is more written about the 1912 elections than the previous ones, an examination of these will demonstrate Lenin's approach to election campaigns and to participation of the Bolsheviks in capitalist parliaments. Unlike the elections in 1906 and 1907, the 1912 elections were held during a rapidly growing upsurge of the working-class movement. Consequently, the opportunities existed for a larger propaganda offensive than in the previous elections. A significantly larger campaign was possible. In 1911, one year before the elections were to take place, Lenin wrote an article entitled "The Election Campaign and the Election Platform" which says in its opening paragraph: "The elections to the Fourth Duma are due to be held next year. The Social Democratic Party must launch its election campaign *at once*. . . . Intensified propaganda, agitation, and organization are on the order of the day, and the forthcoming elections provide a natural, inevitable, topical 'pretext' for such work."[4] In other words, the election campaign was to be the center of the party's propaganda offensive.

Lenin then goes on to explain the importance of the election platform. It is not created especially for election times, but flows from the general program of the party and the positions that the party has established through the experience of previous years. Then he states:

> Very often it may be useful, and sometimes even essential, to give the election platform of social democracy a finishing touch by adding a brief general slogan, a watchword for the

4. V.I. Lenin, "The Election Campaign and the Election Platform," *Collected Works* (hereafter *CW*) (Moscow: Progress Publishers, 1960–70), vol. 17, p. 278.

elections, stating the most cardinal issues of current political practice, and providing a most convenient and most immediate pretext, as well as subject matter, for comprehensive socialist propaganda. In our epoch only the following three points can make up this watchword, this general slogan: (1) a republic, (2) confiscation of all landed estates, and (3) the eight-hour day.[5]

These were the Bolshevik election slogans. These were the demands that the Bolsheviks popularized and took to the masses. In the same way today the Socialist Workers Party focuses on several key demands such as "Bring the Troops Home Now," "Black Control of the Black Community," and "Women's Liberation" in its election platforms.

In January 1912 (the elections were to be held in November), the Bolsheviks adopted an election platform along the lines proposed by Lenin. The initiation of the election campaign coincided with the publication of the first legal Bolshevik newspaper, *Pravda*, a four-page newspaper that came out daily. The launching of *Pravda* was a major victory for the Bolshevik Party. It became the principal instrument for publicizing the election campaign and popularizing its program. Reading the articles Lenin wrote at that time, one can see that he viewed the promotion of *Pravda* and the building of the election campaign as an interlinked process. He wrote comprehensive articles about the paper, discussing how many new subscribers there were, how many were from the working-class districts, etc. Then he analyzed what parts of the country the subscriptions came from, what proportion of subscribers were workers, and so on. He followed the development of the paper very closely along with the development of the election campaign.

At that time the election laws in Russia were extremely restrictive and discriminatory, denying the majority of peasants and

---

5. Lenin, *CW,* vol. 17, p. 281.

workers the vote. They almost make the restrictive election laws of this country seem democratic. In addition, the laws were very complicated and hard to understand. In the section of his biography of Stalin covering this period, Trotsky points out that "combining painstaking attention to details with audacious sweep of thought, Lenin was practically the only Marxist who had thoroughly studied all the possibilities and pitfalls of Stolypin's election laws." Not only was Lenin the party's expert on the election laws, but he was in essence the campaign director. Trotsky writes, "Having politically inspired the election campaign, he guided it technically day by day. To help Petersburg, he sent in from abroad articles and instructions and thoroughly prepared emissaries."[6] That Lenin functioned as campaign director in this manner is particularly amazing, since he was in exile in Poland.

Lenin followed the development of the elections just as he did the growth of the newspaper and the growth of the membership of the party. When the elections were over, he wrote detailed statistical analyses of the meaning of the elections, including the votes that each party received.

In the working-class districts, only Social Democrats were elected, including six Bolsheviks. All six Bolsheviks elected to the fourth Duma were workers, some of whom had been very active in the trade union movement and had played leading roles in it. That was not true of the Mensheviks. Only one or two of their seven deputies were workers.

In the first round of elections, the government used one or another pretext to disqualify workers at a number of factories in St. Petersburg. This triggered huge demonstrations by the workers in support of the right to vote, their right to have an election, and their right to have their own deputies. The Bolsheviks were in the leadership of those demonstrations. As a result, some of the elections in these districts were invalidated and new elections were held. In such a situation, one can safely say, advocates of

---

6. Leon Trotsky, *Stalin* (New York: Stein and Day, 1967), p. 142.

boycotting the elections would not have been too popular among these workers.

The thirteen Social Democratic deputies operated, at least in the beginning stages of participation in the Duma, as a common caucus. On the opening day of the first session of the fourth Duma, the joint caucus refused to participate in the selection of a presiding committee and a presiding chairman. This action was indicative of the policy that the Bolshevik deputies were to take for the next two-and-a-half years. They spoke on the floor, introduced exposés about the conditions of the working class, demanded answers from various government ministers about why things weren't being done better or differently, and participated in committees. But they did not help work on legislation or pass laws. On almost all the bills that came before the Duma, they abstained from the vote. When occasionally a law was introduced that would have a certain benefit for the working class, they would vote for it. But that occurred very, very rarely in the reactionary Duma.

Although the Bolshevik deputies were continually harassed, sometimes suspended from sessions, occasionally arrested, usually interrupted and heckled when speaking on the Duma floor, and continually tailed by the tsarist police, they were still able to function. All the Duma deputies of all parties were supposed to have immunity from arrest; they could only be convicted by a trial of their peers, that is, by the Duma itself. But the government continuously tested to see if it could violate the immunity of the Bolshevik deputies. When the government tried this, however, the masses would intervene with demonstrations and limit the power of the government. Any infringement of the rights of the Bolshevik deputies had a profound radicalizing effect on workers who sincerely believed that their deputies should not suffer such indignities. The Bolshevik deputies had continuous contact with the workers in the factories. They visited the factories, and workers sent delegations to the deputies' headquarters. Badayev, one of the Bolshevik deputies, wrote many years later: "There was not a single factory or workshop, down to the smallest, with which I was not connected in some way or other."[7]

Between sessions of the Duma, the Bolshevik deputies extensively toured all the working-class areas—talking to workers, gathering information and, above all, doing internal party work. It is important to remember that at this time the Bolshevik Party was underground. Even a small liberal bourgeois party, the Cadets, was officially illegal, although it didn't operate underground. The Bolshevik Party could not operate as a legal political party. But its deputies in the Duma, whose members had a certain measure of legal standing, immunity from arrest, and a certain respect—not only respect, but real authority among masses of workers—were in a strategic position to do party work. They could do certain kinds of work much more easily than members who were underground. They helped arrange false passports, set up conferences, raised funds, and worked on the newspaper. Badayev describes how Lenin urged him to work on the newspaper and do internal party work. He describes a myriad of such assignments that these Bolshevik deputies carried out. Their main responsibility was not passing legislation but carrying out a large number of other activities that would be the normal function of any revolutionary party.

Lenin not only played the principal role in inspiring and organizing the election campaign, but he also played a key role in the activity of the Bolshevik fraction in the Duma. There were several meetings in Kraków between the Central Committee members of the party and the Duma deputies to discuss what should be done. Badayev recounts the results of one of these meetings: "We returned from Kraków, armed with concrete practical instructions. The general policy to be followed by the 'six' was clearly outlined and also the details as to who was to speak on various questions, the material that should be prepared, the immediate work to be done outside the Duma, etc. Coming, as

---

7. A. Badayev, *The Bolsheviks in the Tsarist Duma* (New York: Internationaal Publishers, 1929), p. 86.

we did, from an entirely complicated and hostile environment, this direct exchange of ideas with the leading members of the party and above all with Lenin was of the utmost importance for us."[8]

When the Bolshevik deputies were first elected to the Duma, Lenin sent each of them a long questionnaire with questions probing nearly every aspect of the election campaign: how much support had they received from this faction or that faction; how many intellectuals supported them; how many workers supported them; what issues were raised besides those that were in the election platform; how were the various parts of the party platform accepted; what were the arguments that were raised by the workers; what were the questions that were raised? He said, in effect, "I want each of you to fill out a questionnaire so that we can decide what we should do next and how to improve our work in the Duma."

Krupskaya, a leading Bolshevik who was also Lenin's wife, writes in her memoirs that Lenin sometimes drafted the speeches that the deputies gave in the Duma.[9] She recounts some of the speeches, particularly those on education and on the situation in the schools in Russia. It's interesting to look over these speeches because the speeches Lenin wrote for deputies in the Duma were quite different from most of the articles he wrote for *Pravda* or the letters that he sent to party members. He wrote each in a way that could be understood by the people he was trying to reach.

Very little coverage was granted in the bourgeois press to the Bolshevik deputies and of course there was no television or radio then. The only way that a speech in the Duma could be widely circulated to the workers was by publishing it as a pamphlet, printing excerpts of it as a leaflet, or printing it in *Pravda*. Since forty thousand copies of *Pravda* were sold every day in the working-class districts of St. Petersburg, that was the principal way

8. Badayev, *Bolsheviks in the Tsarist Duma*, p. 64.
9. N.K. Krupskaya, *Reminiscences of Lenin* (New York: International Publishers, 1960), p. 256.

the speeches got out. To hear what their deputies were saying in the Duma was a good reason for the workers to buy the paper. In the eyes of the workers, they weren't just Bolshevik deputies, but were looked on as the *workers'* deputies. That was a common phrase in all the propaganda language of the time, *the workers' deputies.* That's how the Bolsheviks referred to their deputies, and that's how the workers referred to them.

As in any parliamentary fraction, the Bolshevik deputies were strongly susceptible to the pressures of adapting to the parliamentary environment. There were more than a few instances when Lenin wrote to them, urging them to take a sharper position on major questions. This was particularly true when the First World War broke out in 1914.

This wasn't the only problem the Bolshevik deputies faced. At the time they were elected, they had been working together in a joint Duma caucus with the Mensheviks. But political differences between the Mensheviks and the Bolsheviks, not only in the Duma caucus, but in the party as a whole, had become so sharp that within a year after the elections the Bolshevik deputies formed their own caucus. In the joint Duma caucus the Menshevik deputies attempted to muzzle the six Bolshevik deputies by placing them under "majority" discipline. A definitive split occurred between the Mensheviks and Bolsheviks that was never healed.

This split had to be explained to the class-conscious workers, and a massive campaign was launched to solicit the support of the workers: collection of petitions; debates at factories between Bolshevik and Menshevik deputies; articles in *Pravda,* and so on. In other words, the position of the Bolshevik deputies was used to expose the Mensheviks before the masses, to drive a wedge between the masses and the Mensheviks, and this they did very successfully. They pointed out that the Mensheviks more and more wanted to adapt to the liberals on this or that question. They wrote about it in their paper and they talked to the workers about it, and within a few weeks it became crystal clear that the Bolsheviks enjoyed far more support among the workers than the

Mensheviks. Badayev estimates that among the class-conscious workers, the Bolsheviks had between 75 and 90 percent of the support; the Mensheviks, the rest. For example, the Bolsheviks held a majority of seats on the boards of fourteen of the eighteen major trade unions in Russia at the time.

Another problem was that a Bolshevik deputy, Roman Malinovsky—the head of the fraction, in fact—was a police agent; he was tsarist cop. In his position, he was of course responsible for the persecution and imprisonment of many Bolsheviks, including the execution of many. But because of the disciplined manner in which the fraction functioned, he was forced to speak for the line of the Bolshevik Party. When, at first, he tried to deviate a little from the line, to soften his position on this or that question a little, Lenin would quickly note it, and he'd be brought to order quickly by the fraction. Malinovsky became one of the best speakers—if not the best speaker—for the Bolsheviks. He was one of the best, most aggressive and outgoing speakers for the Bolsheviks in the Duma and he did a lot of good propaganda work. He was forced to because of the way the fraction operated and the way the party operated. This shows that a disciplined party can't easily be destroyed by police agents.

While Malinovsky was still a deputy, there was a shift in the hierarchy of the police department and his superiors decided to pull him out. Suddenly one day, he left. The Bolsheviks had no warning whatsoever. There had been a few suspicions that he might be a cop, but basically there was no warning. He just took off to some other country. Of course, the fact that he just left like that created a big scandal and the Bolsheviks had to be able to answer it. They denounced him and kicked him out of the party. But there was still no proof that Malinovsky was an agent. It was never proved until after the revolution when the Bolsheviks obtained the tsarist police files. When he returned to Russia after the revolution, he was executed for his role as a police agent.

So we see that one of the best examples of a parliamentary fraction of a socialist party was worked out by the Bolsheviks.

They did it in spite of tremendous obstacles, despite a poor objective situation, and despite the fact that the head of the fraction was a police agent. That's a lot better than what the German socialist movement was able to do at that time under much more auspicious conditions.

With the outbreak of the First World War and the entry of Russia into the war, the Bolshevik deputies held firm in refusing to vote for war credits in the Duma. They voted against the war credits and walked out of the session. First they acted jointly with the Mensheviks; later they held fast by themselves as the Mensheviks capitulated to the pressures. They denounced the imperialist war of their own imperialist ruling class on the floor of the tsarist Duma. Of course, with this position, it was only a matter of a few months before all five of the Bolshevik deputies (not the agent) and six other Bolshevik leaders in the country were arrested, tried, and sentenced to hard labor in Siberia.

Despite the hysterical chauvinism that was sweeping the country and the tightening hold of the governmental reaction, the arrest and trial stimulated worker and student demonstrations and protests. There were protests in the factories against the sentencing of the worker deputies. News of the trial swept throughout the country, leaflets were distributed by the thousands, and the Bolshevik opposition to and explanation of the war were widely communicated.

We should note the kind of defense campaign the Bolsheviks waged. They launched a *massive* defense campaign to get the issues out to the country. The fact that the elected mass leaders of the working class were being sent to Siberia had a profound impact on the consciousness of those who still had parliamentary illusions. (Lenin wrote an article after the trials criticizing most of the deputies for not more clearly stating their position on the war, but praising the good tactics that were used in the defense.)

What are the lessons of these two-and-a-half years of experience? The campaign and election of Duma deputies provided legitimacy and important legal opportunities for the under-ground, illegal Bolshevik Party. It served as a means of reaching and cementing ties with the mass of workers. It served to expose the tsarist government and political parties as well as the liberals and Mensheviks. In particular, it helped to draw a sharp line of distinction between the Bolshevik Party and the reformist Mensheviks. It showed that revolutionaries can use the parliamentary tribune without becoming corrupted, or being maneuvered into taking responsibility for the reactionary government and its policies. Parliamentary work can be merged with, and play a central role in, the entire scope of party activities. Lenin did not view electoral work in a period of ascending radicalization as a peripheral or sideline activity. It was not a task to be carried on in routine fashion; rather, it was the central task of the party, requiring a tremendous mobilization of forces, political inspiration, and great care for detail.

The parliamentary caucus, in order to maintain its principled line and to be effective, must be subordinate to the party as a whole. This was crucial. The Mensheviks and the Western European Social Democratic parliamentary representatives at that time had begun to decide for themselves what their line in parliament was going to be. But the Bolsheviks proved that the only way to maintain a revolutionary perspective in this kind of activity was to keep the Duma caucus, with all the pressures on it, subordinate to the party as a whole.

One of the key lessons was the relationship of this work to the February and October 1917 revolutions. Trotsky writes in his *History of the Russian Revolution* that had a revolutionary situation developed in 1914—and it was possible then—the Bolsheviks might have come directly to power without the country having to go through a provisional government and a Menshevik-Social Revolutionary coalition government with the capitalist parties, as occurred in 1917.

He points out that because of the First World War, national chauvinism, and the victimization of their party, the Bolsheviks were not in a position to seize power during the February 1917 revolution. He then explains that it was those class-conscious workers who had assimilated the lessons and the teachings of the Bolshevik Party two or three years before the outbreak of the war who played a key role in making the February revolution. In 1912–14 the Bolshevik Party was the mass party in the working-class districts. The lessons absorbed in that prewar period—the election campaigns, the participation of the Bolsheviks in the Duma, the things they said in their speeches, the publication of *Pravda*—were crucial in February 1917.

After the February revolution, when the Bolshevik leaders returned from exile, many of the roots they had in the masses before the war still existed, and this facilitated the process of rebuilding the party for the October revolution. There was a direct link between the activity that the Bolshevik Party carried out in the 1912–14 period and the making of the October revolution.

There is another chapter in the history of the Bolshevik approach to electoral activity: their attitude toward the election of the Constituent Assembly in 1917. The Provisional Government that was thrown up after the tsarist regime was ousted in the February revolution continually promised to call a Constituent Assembly, but in practice kept delaying it. The Bolsheviks supported a Constituent Assembly because there were still widespread illusions, particularly among the peasants, about the necessity for an assembly, i.e., a bourgeois republican form of government; and these illusions had to be dispelled.

The Bolsheviks' vigorous support for a Constituent Assembly helped expose the reluctance of the bourgeois parties and the reformists to call elections for the Constituent Assembly. Although the Bolsheviks supported a Constituent Assembly against the restoration of the monarchy or a military coup d'état they left no doubt that between a workers republic based on soviets and a bourgeois parliamentary republic they favored the former.

When elections for a Constituent Assembly were finally called, the Bolsheviks participated in them. Lists of candidates had to be drawn up and submitted to the electoral commission by October 17. Elections were scheduled for November 12. Between these dates, the Soviets, under the leadership of the Bolshevik Party, took political power. There was a social revolution, the most momentous in the history of the world. This posed the question: should the Bolsheviks cancel the elections for the Constituent Assembly scheduled for November 12? The Bolsheviks decided to permit the elections and keep their own candidates in the race.

When the Constituent Assembly met the first week in January 1918, two months after the new Soviet government came to power, the Bolsheviks introduced a resolution in the Assembly calling on the body to support the Soviet government. The Bolsheviks did not have a majority, and when the delegates voted this motion down, exposing where they really stood as opponents of the workers government, the Bolsheviks dissolved the Constituent Assembly in the name of the Soviet government. By this time, after two months of revolution and experience, and because of the stand of the other reformist parties on the question of the Soviet government, most of the illusions of the masses about parliamentarism had been dispelled.

Reviewing this experience later in "'Left-Wing' Communism, an Infantile Disorder," Lenin wrote:

> The conclusion which follows from this is absolutely incontrovertible: it has been proved that, far from causing harm to the revolutionary proletariat, participation in a bourgeois-democratic parliament, even a few weeks before the victory of a Soviet republic and even *after* such a victory, actually helps that proletariat to *prove* to the backward masses why such parliaments deserve to be done away with; it *facilitates* their successful dissolution, and *helps* to make bourgeois parliamentarism "politically obsolete."[10]

---

10. Lenin, "'Left-Wing' Communism, an Infantile Disorder," *Collected Works*, vol. 31, p. 60.

The positive lessons of the Bolshevik experience in parliamentarism, along with the negative example of the Western European parties, was discussed thoroughly and codified in a set of theses adopted at the Second Congress of the Communist International in 1920. In summary, some of the key points included in these theses are:

• Bourgeois parliaments or congresses cannot in any way serve as the arena of struggle for reform, or for improving the lot of the working people.

• Revolutionary socialists repudiate parliamentarism, as a state form, for the class dictatorship of the working class. They repudiate the possibility of winning over parliament to their side. It is only possible to speak of utilizing the capitalist state organization with the object of destroying it.

• The fundamental method of struggle of the working class against capitalist rule is the method of mass action; parliamentary tactics, although important, are supplementary and subordinate.

• The objective of work within elections or capitalist congresses is propaganda to reach workers and other sectors of the population who have not yet been reached.

• Election campaigns should not be geared primarily toward getting votes, but should be revolutionary mobilizations involving not only the party leaders and candidates but the entire party membership.

• Refusal to participate in elections in principle is a naive, childish doctrine.

• The question of the form of intervention in elections, including boycotts, is a tactical question, to be worked out according to the concrete circumstances.

These theses were discussed and passed because of the strong tendency in many of the new, militant but inexperienced Communist parties adhering to the Third International to reject all forms of parliamentarism and all participation in any type of legal organization such as trade unions.

I would like to conclude by referring to Lenin's attitude toward election campaigns in Western Europe and the United States. He stated that he knew people said that this form of parliamentarism was fine in Russia, but that in other countries things were different. That was the wrong conclusion, Lenin said. Communists in all countries should:

> exist for the purpose of *changing*—all along the line, in all spheres of life—the old socialist, trade unionist, syndicalist, and parliamentary type of work into a *new* type of work, the communist. In Russia, too, there was always an abundance of opportunism, purely bourgeois sharp practices and capitalist rigging in the elections. In Western Europe and in America, the Communists must learn to create a new, uncustomary, non-opportunist, and non-careerist parliamentarianism; the Communist parties must issue their slogans; true proletarians, with the help of the unorganized and downtrodden poor, should distribute leaflets, canvass workers' houses and cottages of the rural proletarians and peasants in the remote villages . . . ; they should go into the public houses, penetrate into unions, societies, and chance gatherings of the common people, and speak to the people, not in learned (or very parliamentary) language; they should not at all strive to "get seats" in parliament, but should everywhere try to get people to think, and draw the masses into the struggle, to take the bourgeoisie at its word and utilize the machinery it has set up, the elections it has appointed, and the appeals it has made to the people; they should try to explain to the people what Bolshevism is, in a way that was never possible (under bourgeois rule) outside of election times (exclusive, of course, of times of big strikes, when in Russia a *similar* apparatus for widespread popular agitation worked even more intensively). It is very difficult . . . ; but it can and must be done, for the objectives of communism cannot be achieved without effort. We must work to accomplish *practical* tasks, ever more var-

ied and ever more closely connected with all branches of social life, *winning* branch after branch, and sphere after sphere *from the bourgeoisie.*[11]

---

11. Lenin, "'Left-Wing' Communism," *CW,* vol. 31, pp. 98–99.

from Pathfinder

Capitalism's World Disorder
Working-Class Politics at the Millennium
JACK BARNES

The social devastation and financial panic, the coarsening of politics and politics of resentment, the cop brutality and acts of imperialist aggression accelerating around us—all are the product of lawful forces unleashed by capitalism. But the future the propertied classes have in store for us can be changed by the united struggle and selfless action of workers and farmers conscious of their power to transform the world. $23.95. Also available in Spanish and French.

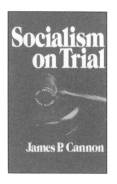

Cuba and the Coming American Revolution
JACK BARNES

"There will be a victorious revolution in the United States before there will be a victorious counterrevolution in Cuba." That statement, made by Fidel Castro in 1961, remains as accurate today as when it was spoken. This is a book about the class struggle in the United States, where the revolutionary capacities of workers and farmers are today as utterly discounted by the ruling powers as were those of the Cuban toilers. And just as wrongly. It is about the example set by the people of Cuba that revolution is not only necessary—it can be made. $13.00

Socialism on Trial
JAMES P. CANNON

The basic ideas of socialism, explained in testimony during the trial of 18 leaders of the Minneapolis Teamsters union and the Socialist Workers Party framed up and imprisoned under the notorious Smith "Gag" Act during World War II. $15.95

The Communist Manifesto

KARL MARX AND FREDERICK ENGELS

Founding document of the modern working-class movement, published in 1848. Explains why communism is derived not from preconceived principles but from facts, from proletarian movements springing from the actual class struggle. $3.95. Also available in Spanish.

Lenin's Final Fight

Speeches and Writings, 1922–23

V.I. LENIN

In the early 1920s Lenin waged a political battle in the leadership of the Communist Party of the USSR to maintain the course that had enabled the workers and peasants to overthrow the tsarist empire, carry out the first successful socialist revolution, and begin building a world communist movement. The issues posed in Lenin's political fight remain at the heart of world politics today. $19.95. Also available in Spanish.

Che Guevara Talks to Young People

The legendary Argentine-born revolutionary challenges youth of Cuba and the world to work and become disciplined. To fearlessly join the front lines of struggles, small and large. To read and to study. To aspire to be revolutionary combatants. To politicize the organizations they are part of and in the process politicize themselves. To become a different kind of human being as they strive together with working people of all lands to transform the world. And, along this line of march, to renew and revel in the spontaneity and joy of being young. $14.95. Also available in Spanish.

To Speak the Truth

Why Washington's 'Cold War' against Cuba Doesn't End

FIDEL CASTRO AND CHE GUEVARA

In historic speeches before the United Nations and UN bodies, Guevara and Castro address the workers of the world, explaining why the U.S. government so hates the example set by the socialist revolution in Cuba and why Washington's effort to destroy it will fail. $16.95

Malcolm X Speaks

Speeches from the last year of Malcolm X's life tracing the evolution of his views on racism, capitalism, socialism, political action, and more. $17.95. Also available in Spanish.

U.S. Hands off the Mideast!

Cuba Speaks out at the United Nations

FIDEL CASTRO, RICARDO ALARCON

The case against Washington's 1990–91 embargo and war against Iraq, as presented by the Cuban government at the United Nations. $10.95. Also available in Spanish.

Aspects of Socialist Election Policy

Documents and articles on the communist approach to electoral work. Includes theses on parliamentary reformism adopted at the Second Congress of the Communist International, the nature of the capitalist two-party system, and the fight for independent political action by labor and oppressed nationalities. $10.00

The Jewish Question

A Marxist Interpretation

ABRAM LEON

Traces the historical rationalizations of anti-Semitism to the fact that Jews — in the centuries preceding the domination of industrial capitalism — were forced to become a "people-class" of merchants and moneylenders. Leon explains why the propertied rulers incite renewed Jew-hatred today. $17.95

Feminism and the Marxist Movement

MARY-ALICE WATERS

Since the founding of the modern revolutionary workers movement nearly 150 years ago, Marxists have championed the struggle for women's rights and explained the economic roots in class society of women's oppression. $3.00

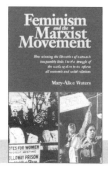